THIS BLOOMSBURY BOOK

BELONGS TO

....

Bloomsbury Book of Lullabies

Selected by Belinda Hollyer

Illustrated by Robin Bell Corfield

BLOOMSBURY
CHILDREN'S
BOOKS

The evening is coming

The evening is coming, the sun sinks to rest,
The birds are all flying straight home to their nests,
"Caw, caw," says the crow as he flies overhead,
It's time little children were going to bed.

Here comes the pony, his work is all done,
Down through the meadow he takes a good run,
Up go his heels — and down goes his head.
It's time little children were going to bed.

Bedtime

Five minutes, five minutes more please!
   Let me stay five minutes more!
Can't I just finish the castle
   I'm building here on the floor?
Can't I just finish the story
   I'm reading here in my book?
Can't I just finish this bead-chain –
   It *almost* is finished, look!
Can't I just finish this game, please?
   When a game's once begun
It's a pity never to find out
   Whether you've lost or won.
Can't I just stay five minutes?
   Well, can't I stay just four?
Three minutes then? two minutes?
   Can't I stay just *one* minute more?

Eleanor Farjeon

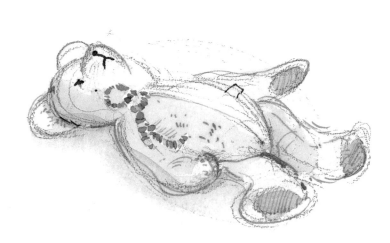

Go to bed, Tom

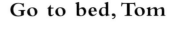

Go to bed, Tom,
Go to bed, Tom,
Tired or not, Tom.
Go to bed, Tom.

Getting-ready-lullaby

Hug me gentle, hug me strong,
hug me short and hug me long.
Now it's time to put away
all the pieces of today –
all the games and all the toys,
all the bother and the noise,
all the girls and all the boys –
back they go into their box
till tomorrow morning knocks.

Now a bath for sleepyhead,
then it's story time in bed,
then once more it's hug-me-tight,
kisses, and turn out the light.

Russell Hoban

Down with the lambs

Down with the lambs
Up with the lark,
Run to bed children
Before it gets dark.

Go to bed late

Go to bed late
  Stay very small;
Go to bed early
  Grow very tall.

I see the moon

I see the moon
And the moon sees me;
God bless the moon
And God bless me.

In jumping and tumbling

In jumping and tumbling
We spend the whole day,
Till night by arriving
Has finished our play.

What then? One and all,
There's no more to be said,
As we tumbled all day,
So we tumble to bed.

You be saucer

You be saucer,
I'll be cup,
piggyback, piggyback
pick me up.

You be tree,
I'll be pears,
carry me, carry me
up the stairs.

You be Good,
I'll be Night,
tuck me in, tuck me in
nice and tight.

Eve Merriam

Ten, nine, eight

10 small toes all washed and warm
9 soft friends in a quiet room
8 square windowpanes with falling snow
7 empty shoes in a short straight row
6 pale seashells hanging down
5 round buttons on a yellow gown
4 sleepy eyes which open and close
3 loving kisses on cheeks and nose
2 strong arms around a fuzzy bear's head
1 big girl all ready for bed

Molly Bang

Good night

Now good night.
  Fold up your clothes
  As you were taught,
  Fold your two hands,
  Fold up your thought;
  Day is the plough-land,
  Night is the stream,
  Day is for doing
  And night is for dream.
Now good night.

Eleanor Farjeon

God bless this house from thatch to floor

God bless this house from thatch to floor,
The twelve apostles guard the door
Four angels to my bed;
Gabriel stands at the head,
John and Peter at my feet,
All to watch me while I sleep.

Dance to your daddy

Dance to your daddy
My little babby,
Dance to your daddy
My little lamb

You shall have a fishy
In a little dishy,
You shall have a fishy
When the boat comes in.

Hushabye my darling

Hushabye my darling
Don't you make a peep
Little creatures everywhere
Are settling down to sleep

Fishes in the millpond
Goslings in the barn
Kitten by the fireside
Baby in my arms

Listen to the raindrops
Singing you to sleep
Hushabye my darling
Don't you make a peep

Clyde Watson

Where do you sleep?

The green worm sleeps in silk,
The turtle sleeps in sand,
And the bluebird sleeps in a feather bed,
The yak prefers to stand.
The white lamb sleeps in wool,
The ermine sleeps in fur,
But the monkey sleeps in his mummy's arms,
All warm and close to her.

William Engvick

Dream-song

Sunlight, moonlight,
Twilight, starlight –
Gloaming at the close of day,
And an owl calling,
Cool dews falling
In a wood of oak and may.

Lantern-light, taper-light,
Torchlight, no-light:
Darkness at the shut of day,
And lions roaring,
Their wrath pouring
In wild waste places far away.

Elf-light, bat-light,
Touchwood-light and toad-light,
And the sea a shimmering gloom of grey,
And a small face smiling
In a dream's beguiling
In a world of wonders far away.

Walter de la Mare

The mother sings

Rockaby, my baby,
Slumber if you can.
I wonder what you're going to be
When you're grown a man.

If you are a monarch
On a gold and silver throne,
With all the lands of East and West
For to call your own,
I know you'll be the greatest monarch
Ever was known.

If you are a poet
With the magic of the word,
A swan's quill to write with
And a voice like a bird,
I know you'll be the greatest poet
Ever was heard.

But whether you're a monarch
And make your bride a queen,
Or whether you're a poet
With men's hearts to glean,
I know you are the sweetest baby
Ever was seen.

Rockaby, my baby,
Slumber if you can.
I wonder what you're going to be
When you're grown a man.

Eleanor Farjeon

Gaelic Lullaby

Hush! the waves are rolling in,
   White with foam, white with foam;
Father toils amid the din;
   But baby sleeps at home.

Hush! the winds roar hoarse and deep,
   On they come, on they come!
Brother seeks the wandering sheep;
   But baby sleeps at home.

Hush! the rain sweeps over the knowes,
   Where they roam, where they roam;
Sister goes to seek the cows;
   But baby sleeps at home.

Oh father's at the sea

Oh father's at the sea,
  baby mine,
Oh father's at the sea,
  baby mine,
And you're all I've got,
Here asleeping in your cot,
  Such a blessed little dot,
  baby mine.

Thomas E Brown

The Sounds in the Evening

The sounds in the evening
Go all through the house,
The click of the clock
And the pick of the mouse,
The footsteps of people
Upon the top floor,
The skirts of my mother
That brush by my door,
The crick in the boards,
And the creak of the chairs,
The fluttering murmurs
Outside on the stairs,
The ring at the bell,
The arrival of guests,
The laugh of my father
At one of his jests,
The clashing of dishes
As dinner goes in,
The babble of voices
That distance makes thin,
The mewings of cats
That seem just by my ear,
The hooting of owls
That can never seem near,
The queer little noises
That no one explains –
Till the moon through the slats
Of my window-blind rains,
And the world of my eyes
And my ears melts like steam
As I find in my pillow
The world of my dream.

Eleanor Farjeon

Night sounds

In the street
  sounds of wheels humming,
   sounds of heels drumming.
Humming and drumming,
Keeping me from sleeping.
In the house
  sounds of words mumbling,
   overheard grumbling.
Mumbling and grumbling,
Keeping me unsleeping.
Far away
  sounds of waves lashing,
   quietly crashing.
Lashing and crashing,
Sweeping me to sleep.

Felice Holman

Evening

Hush, hush, little baby,
   The sun's in the west;
The lamb in the meadow
   Has laid down to rest.

The bough rocks the bird now,
   The flower rocks the bee,
The wave rocks the lily,
   The wind rocks the tree;

And I rock the baby
   So softly to sleep –
It must not awaken
   Till daisy-buds peep.

Lullaby

The moon and the stars and the wind in the sky
All night long sing a lullaby,
While down in the ocean so dark and so deep
The silvery waves rock the fishes to sleep.

Jean Jaszi

All tucked in & roasty toasty

All tucked in & roasty toasty
Blow me a kiss good-night
Close your eyes till morning comes
Happy dreams & sleep tight

Clyde Watson

Are all the giants dead?

Are all the giants dead?
And all the witches fled?
Am I quite safe in bed?

Giants and witches all are fled.
My child, thou art quite safe in bed.

A spell for sleeping

Sweet william, silverweed, sally-my-handsome.
Dimity darkens the pittering water.
On gloomed lawns wanders a king's daughter.
Curtains are clouding the casement windows.
A moon-glade smurrs the lake with light.
Doves cover the tower with quiet.

Three owls whit-whit in the withies.
Seven fish in a deep pool shimmer.
The princess moves to the spiral stair.

Slowly the sickle moon mounts up.
Frogs hump under moss and mushroom.
The princess climbs to her high hushed room,

Step by step to her shadowed tower.
Water laps the white lake shore.
A ghost opens the princess' door.

Seven fish in the sway of the water.
Six candles for a king's daughter.
Five sighs for a drooping head.
Four ghosts to gentle her bed.
Three owls in the dusk falling.
Two tales to be telling.
One spell for sleeping.

Tamarisk, trefoil, tormentil.
Sleep rolls down from the clouded hill.
A princess dreams of a silver pool.

The moonlight spreads, the soft ferns flit
Stilled in a shimmering drift of water,
Seven fish dream of a lost king's daughte

Alastair Reid

Once, a lullaby

Once I was a little horse,
baby horse, little horse.
Once I was a little horse.
Neigh, I fell asleep.

Once I was a little cow,
baby cow, little cow.
Once I was a little cow.
Moo, I fell asleep.

Once I was a little goat,
baby goat, little goat.
Once I was a little goat.
Maa, I fell asleep.

Once I was a little sheep,
baby sheep, little sheep.
Once I was a little sheep.
Baa, I fell asleep.

Once I was a little dog,
baby dog, little dog.
Once I was a little dog.
Arf, I fell asleep.

Once I was a little owl,
baby owl, little owl.
Once I was a little owl,
Whoo, I went to sleep.

And then:
bee – **bzzz**
boy – **waa**
chick – **cheep**
crow – **caw**
duck – **quack**
fish – **glub**
fly – **hmmm**
frog – **croak**
girl – **waa**

bp Nichol

Once I was a little mouse,
baby mouse, little mouse.
Once I was a little mouse.
Squeak, I went to sleep.

Lullaby

Sh sh what do you wish
sh sh the windows are shuttered
sh sh a magical fish
swims out from the window and down to the river

lap lap the waters are lapping
sh sh the shore slips away
glide glide glide with the current
sh sh the shadows are deeper

sleep sleep tomorrow is sure

Eve Merriam

Pillow song

Moony, moony, silver deep
ocean rock me to my sleep
Morning sunshine in my cup,
sing a song to wake me up.

Russell Hoban

Catch me the moon, Daddy

Catch me the moon, Daddy,
Let it shine near me for a while,
Catch me the moon, Daddy,
I want to touch its smile.

The moon must shine from high above;
That's where it needs to stay
Among the stars, to guide them home
When they return from play.

So the bunny can find his supper,
So the mouse can scamper free,
So the hedgehog can make his forays,
So the birds can sleep in the tree.

And as for you, my child,
With slender silver thread
The moon will weave sweet dreams, so you
May slumber in your bed.

Grigor Vitez

The white seal's lullaby

Oh! hush thee, my baby, the night is behind us,
  And black are the waters that sparkled so green.
The moon, o'er the combers, looks downward to find us
  At rest in the hollows that rustle between.
Where billow meets billow, then soft be thy pillow;
  Ah, weary wee flipperling, curl at thy ease!
The storm shall not wake thee, nor shark overtake thee,
  Asleep in the arms of the slow-swinging seas.

Rudyard Kipling

Copyright acknowledgements

The compiler and publisher would like to thank the following for permission to reprint the poems in this book. All possible care has been taken to trace the ownership of the poems included, and to make full acknowledgement of their use. Any errors or omissions which have accidentally occurred despite those efforts will be corrected in subsequent editions if notification is sent to the publisher.

Page 8 'Bedtime' by Eleanor Farjeon, from *Silver, Sand and Snow* by Eleanor Farjeon and published by Michael Joseph 1951, reprinted by permission of David Higham Associates Ltd

Page 9 'Getting-ready-lullaby' by Russell Hoban, © Russell Hoban 1996, reprinted by permission of David Higham Associates Ltd

Page 12 'You be saucer' by Eve Merriam, from *Out Loud*, reprinted by permission of William Morrow & Company

Page 14 'Ten, nine, eight' by Molly Bang, from *Ten, nine, eight* © 1983 Molly Bang, reprinted by permission of Walker Books Ltd

Page 14 'Good night' by Eleanor Farjeon, from *Something I Remember* by Eleanor Farjeon, reprinted by permission of David Higham Associates Ltd

Page 18 'Hushabye my darling' by Clyde Watson, from *Catch Me & Kiss Me & Say It Again* © Clyde Watson 1978 published by William Collins Sons & Company, reprinted by permission of Curtis Brown Ltd

Page 19 'Where do you sleep?' by William Engvick from *Lullabies and Nightsongs* edited by William Engvick, © 1965 by Alec Wilder and William Engvick, reprinted by permission of HarperCollins Publishers

Page 21 'Dream-song' by Walter de la Mare from *Peacock Pie* published in 1913, reprinted by permission of the Literary Trustees of Walter de la Mare and The Society of Authors as their representative

Page 22 'The mother sings' by Eleanor Farjeon from *Silver Sand and Snow* by Eleanor Farjeon published by Michael Joseph 1951, reprinted by permission of David Higham Associates Ltd

Page 26 'The sounds in the evening' by Eleanor Farjeon from *Silver Sand and Snow* by Eleanor Farjeon published by Michael Joseph 1951, reprinted by permission of David Higham Associates Ltd

Page 27 'Night sounds' by Felice Holman from *At The Top of My Voice and Other Poems* by Felice Holman, published by Charles Scribner's Sons, © 1970, reprinted by permission of Felice Holman, copyright owner

Page 29 'Lullaby' by Jean Jaszi from *Everybody Has Two Eyes* by Jean Jaszi published by Lothrop, Lee & Shepard Company, reprinted by permission of William Morrow & Company

Page 30 'All tucked in & roasty toasty' by Clyde Watson, from *Catch Me & Kiss Me & Say It Again* © Clyde Watson 1978 published by William Collins Sons & Company, reprinted by permission of Curtis Brown Ltd

Page 34 'A spell for sleeping' by Alastair Reid from *A New Treasury of Poetry* published by Blackie 1990, © Alastair Reid and reprinted by permission of the author

Page 36 'Once, a lullaby' by bp Nichol from *Once, A Lullaby* by bp Nichol published by Greenwillow Books 1986 and reprinted by permission of William Morrow and Company

Page 38 'Lullaby' by Eve Merriam from *Out Loud* by Eve Merriam published by William Morrow and Company and reprinted by permission of the publisher

Page 39 'Pillow song' by Russell Hoban © Russell Hoban 1996, reprinted by permission of David Higham Associates Ltd

Page 40 'Catch me the moon, Daddy' by Griger Vitez from *The UNICEF Book of Children's Poems* edited by Walter Kaufman

First published in Great Britain in 1998 by Bloomsbury Publishing Plc
38 Soho Square, London W1V 5DF

A CIP catalogue record for this book is available from the British Library.
ISBN 0 7475 5014 X (paperback)
ISBN 0 7475 3061 0 (hardback)

Printed in Singapore by Tien Wah Press
Typeset by Stefania Bonelli

1 3 5 7 9 10 8 6 4 2

Design by Herman Lelie

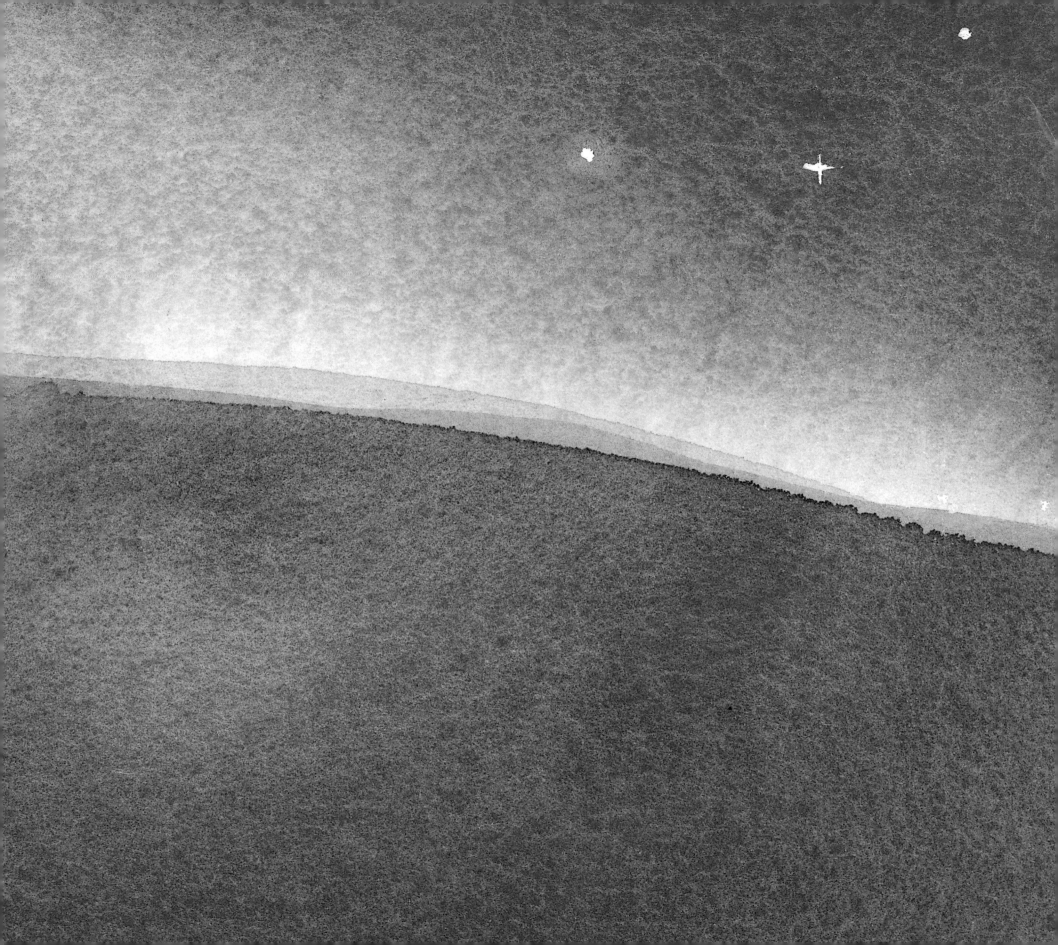

Acclaim for this book

'This sleepy collection of bedtime rhymes and verse is perfectly matched by the dreamy illustrations in pastel watercolours' *Junior*

'Children of today (and their parents) have never had it so good when they can be exposed to books of such stunning beauty ... Robin Bell Corfield's glorious artwork in sunset hues is a joy to behold and each picture richly complements the lyrical text' *The Bookseller*

'This collection is enchanting with its combination of both contemporary and traditional lullabies. The variety of material is refreshing with some magical little-known verses' *Baby Magazine*